navigate

a guidebook for the
lighthouse revolution

karen gunton

navigate by karen gunton karengunton.com

copyright © karen gunton 2017

ISBN 9780994564627

the moral rights of the author have been asserted. the suggestions and opinions of the author are personal views only. the strategies and steps outlined are a guide only. the author in all cases recommends personal due diligence and thorough research. all rights reserved. this book may not be reproduced in whole, part, stored, posted on in the internet or transmitted in any form by any means, electronic, mechanical, photocopying, recording, or other without the written permission from the author and the publisher of this book.

cover image: CC0 public domain pixabay.com author: chriswoehrl
author photo: kelli dudley kellidphotos.com
printed by: ingramspark.com

navigate:

to give direction

to show the way

to guide your journey

table of contents

your lighthouse. your light. 7

the road so far 13

    reflect. 15

    remember. 17

    decide. 19

    contrast. 21

ignite your light. 27

    be you. 29

    your soul purpose. 31

    your BIG vision. 33

    your why. 35

    your spark. 37

    future you. 39

be a beacon 45

    share you. 47

    your comfort zone. 49

    your story. 51

    your signature thing. 53

    your manifesto. 55

    your connections. 57

build your tower 63

    serve you. 65

    your tower. 67

    your permission. 69

    your definitions. 71

    your focus. 73

    your sacred space. 75

table of contents

strengthen your foundation 81
    your foundation. 83
    your responsibility. 85
    your certainty. 87
    your action taking. 89
    your mindset. 91
    your rituals. 93

use the spiral staircase 99
    awareness. 101
    understanding. 103
    clearing. 105
    reframing. 107
    fun. 109
    your tools. 111

find your harbour 117
    your darkness. 119
    your come back rate. 121
    belonging. 123
    safety. 125
    your anchor. 127
    your walls. 129

look up at the sky 135
    your intuition. 137
    your spirituality. 139
    your universe. 141
    your vibes. 143

make like a lighthouse and shine. 149

your lighthouse. your light.

you are here to be the highest, brightest version of yourself... to live a life that lights you up... to shine your light! the best way to shine is to build a lighthouse... to BE a lighthouse.

this guidebook is a companion to the book *lighthouse revolution* (which, if you haven't already read, you can find at lighthouserevolution.com) and explores strategies for building each component of your lighthouse.

the exercises are meant to guide you... they are not set in stone, so feel free to adapt them, use them in your own way, do them in any order you like, come back to them again and again if it helps.

i have included blank space for every exercise... use these blank pages to expand on the exercise, to note some of your own strategies, to record your own quotes or mantras, to brainstorm, dream, or journal...

you can do the guidebook and build your lighthouse for your own personal journey or you can do it with your biz/career in mind... you can think about one aspect of your life or you can do it for your life as a whole... it is up to you!

navigate is about exploring you, it's about finding your way to your light, it's about building your lighthouse your way, and it's about your journey... one that never really ends, and is of course different for everyone.

the lighthouse provides a framework for self-leadership... for rising up by yourself, for yourself... and navigate will take you down that pathway.

so let's make like a lighthouse... and shine!

pull over
to the side of
your journey
and look how
far you've come.

danielle laporte

the road so far

everything you have done so far has led you to where you are right now... which is exactly where you are meant to be.

reflection is not about dwelling on the past, it is about observing it, acknowledging it, understanding it, releasing it... all so that you can feel empowered to move forward.

a look back at where you have been, and how you got here, can help you get clear about where you are going next.

it's a chance to consider what didn't go well and to celebrate what went right. it's a chance to learn and a chance to grow.

you can do your reflection for the year gone by, or you can consider your whole journey so far, or you can even just think about something you've been working on recently. it's up to you.

before you navigate your way towards your light, take some time to reflect on the road so far.

reflect.

what brought you here... to this moment in time... ready to ignite your light and shine?
where have you been? what have you experienced? what has the journey been like for you until now?

the road so far...

remember.

dreams came true

goals achieved

best **memories**

most **proud** of

hardest thing

disappointed you

a **weak** point

biggest **frustration**

AHA! moments

obstacles overcome

fears came up

lessons **learned**

most **grateful** for

inspired you

surprised you

ignited you

decide.

what do you do with your reflection? be intentional with what you take with you and what you let go.

celebrate.
when we celebrate our success we train our brains to believe we are worthy and deserving of success. celebrate BIG and celebrate often!

celebrate achievements, great feedback, results; signs, synchronicities, nudges; times you followed your intuition, purpose, or passion; times you took a leap and great things happened...

release.
release what is holding you back so you can step forward. let go of the stuff that is not serving you or didn't work out.

release failures, flops, disappointments; limiting beleifs, patterns, stories, memories; old strategies, offerings, rituals, activities...

remember.
remember what you have learned and what you choose to take forward with you now.

remember lessons learned; AHAs, signs, messages, signposts along the road; anything you want to keep in mind, any promise you want to make for yourself

contrast.

compare where you've been to where you want to go next... let it help you learn what you want now.

how did you feel?	how do you **want to feel**?
how did you spend your time?	how do you **want to spend your time**?
who did you feel like you needed to be?	who do you **want to be**?

clarity doesn't
always mean
you know exactly
what you are doing.
but it does mean
you know exactly
who you are being,
and why.

christine kane

ignite your light

the first component of the lighthouse is the light. you must get back to your light. because it all starts and ends with your light.

what is the light? where does it come from?

YOU.

your light is you.

the way to ignite your light is simply to BE you.

many of us may first need to find ourselves again. many of us will need to remember who we were before life started to get in the way. some of us will need to give ourselves permission to simply be the person we feel we are inside. some of us will need to spend some time getting to know our selves again.

but when we do... when we can tap into our own souls, with authenticity and clarity, that is when we will begin to feel lit up from within, once again, as we were born to do.

we are each here for a reason, we have our own journey to go on, our own purpose to find and achieve... we have a light we are here to shine.

some ways to ignite your light include: learning you & being you, having a clear vision for what you want in life: your goals & your dreams, finding and following your purpose, knowing what fuels your spark, and more... anything that lights you up and feels like you.

the light is all about awareness, clarity, vision, purpose, and drive.

it's about being you.

be you.

your light is like a beautiful chandelier made up of many facets: this is about seeing yourself clearly... hanging each crystal from your chandelier, allowing your light to shine through your unique YOUness.

you can be many things, you can be more than one thing at once, you can decide you don't want to be something anymore, you can act as if you already are. you decide which pieces you hang on your chandelier. one of the most powerful sentences in the world is "i am." how you follow up those words is up to you... choose wisely.

revisit what you know about you, explore you (try taking an online quiz!), ask your friends "what would you say are my superpowers?" consider your: strengths, personality type, archetypes, values, zone of genius, uniqueness, weirdness...

i am...

your soul purpose.

do you remember who you were born to be? what you were born to do? before the world told you who and what and how you should be? here are some questions to help you explore your purpose.

when you were little what did you **dream** of doing?

what sorts of **signs**, messages, or inner whisperings do you get pointing you in a certain direction?

do you have a mysterious sense that you are just **meant** to do something? what is it?

do you have an idea **deep** down that you don't really let yourself think about?

if you didn't have to **worry** about getting it right what would you do?

what fills you up? makes you feel whole? ignited? most like **you**?

if you knew you were going to die one year from now, what would you **do**?

how do you want to be remembered? what is the **legacy** you want to leave?

what is your biggest **challenge**? (your deepest wound is often your greatest gift!)

what comes **easy** to you, or seems so obvious to you, but doesn't seem so for others?

in what areas of your life do you feel like you are making a **difference**?

what is **calling** to you right now... to take a leap that feels a bit impossible or scary?

how could you **contribute** to saving the world?

your BIG vision.

imagine your future... what do you want to be, do, have, and feel? think BIG. imagine if... you weren't afraid, you couldn't fail, money were no object, the possibilities were endless. consider the secret dream that lives inside of you. create a BIG vision for yourself... this is about claiming your dream!

be.

do.

have.

feel.

your why.

if your vision is where you are going... your why is what drives you there, it pulls you forward (instead of pushing all the time) it's the reason you do what you do.

simon senek says "people don't buy what you do, they buy why you do it." i think YOU also need to buy why you do it... go after what you want by tapping into why you want it.

have a why for each of your goals, have a why for everything you are working towards. and have a BIG why that gets to the core of who you are being, what you are doing, where you are going. if it's hard to put your why into words, try tapping into how it FEELS.

here are some questions to help you dig deeper and get to the core of why.

why **focus** on this?

why is this so **important**?

why **this** and not something else?

why does it **matter**?

why does it make a **difference**?

why does it **excite** you? why does it light you up?

why **fight** for this? why won't you give up on it?

why is this **worth** the work/sacrifice/struggle/effort that it may take?

your spark.

in order to get where we are going, we need some fuel in the tank! think about that chandelier that makes up the light you shine... what turns on your light? we can have many light switches in our life... they do not have to be related to your work or goal, they just need to help you feel like YOU!

what sparks your fire... fills up your tank... ignites you... is essential fuel for you?

future you.

look across the harbour at future you... that highest, brightest you... the lighthouse version of you!

what is she **like**? how does she spend her time? what does she talk about?

what **advice** would she give you? what would she want you to know?

how does future you compare the **role** you have boxed yourself into right now?

in what way can you start **acting as if**? practice, prepare for the role you long to play?

navigate | 39

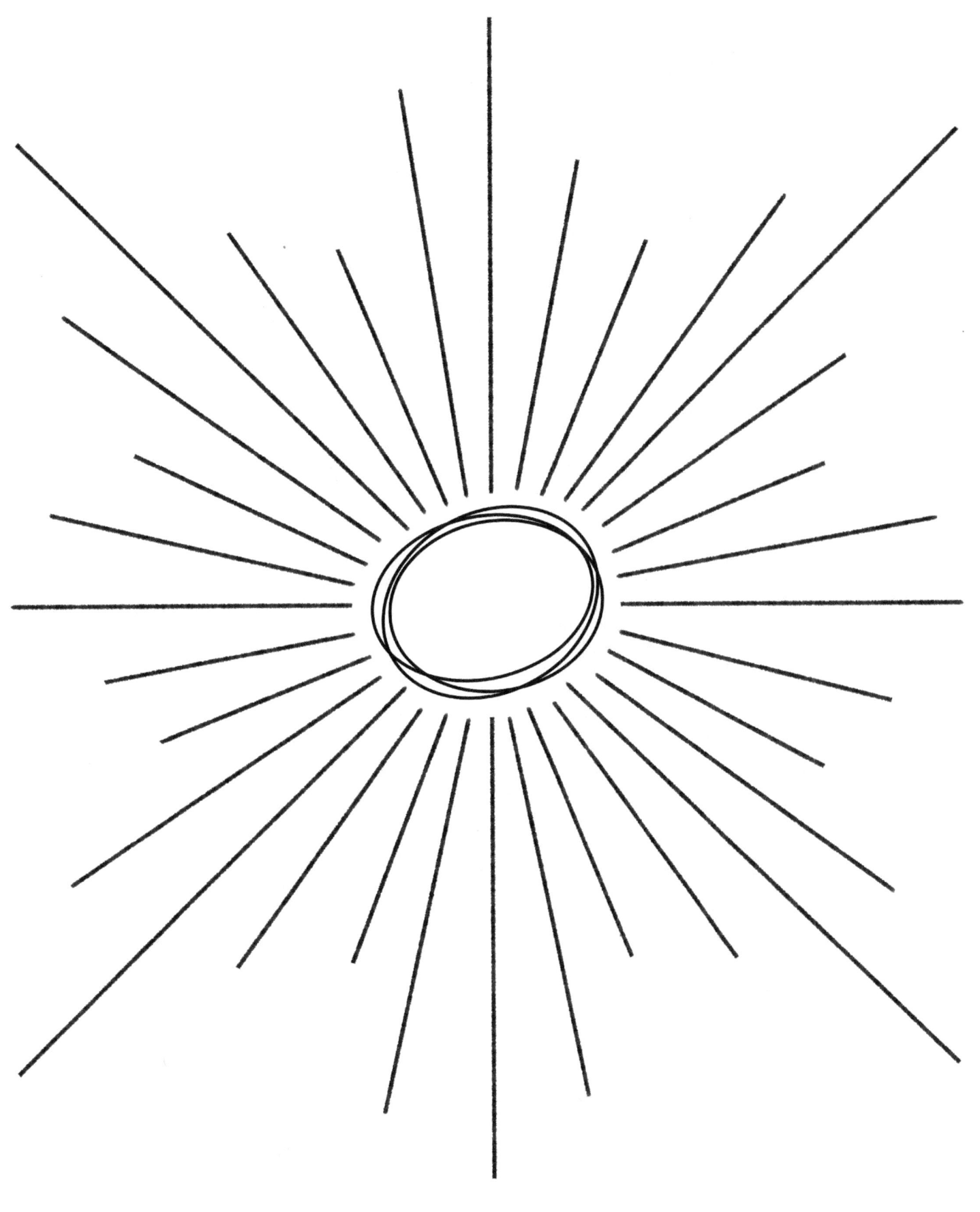

this is how i shine

the one thing
that you have
that nobody else has
is YOU...
your voice, your mind,
your story, your vision.

neil gaimen

be a beacon

the next component of the lighthouse is the beacon.

think about the beacon of a lighthouse... it is a signal, a beam, a message... a guiding light to the boats at sea.

when you shine your light, that is what your light becomes to others... a beacon.

not only are you here to BE you, you are here to SHARE you.

your light is not meant to be hidden inside, dimmed, diminished, or contained... you are not meant to shine quietly or discretely or in isolation.

(if the lighthouse brings to mind a feeling of isolation it is only because you are forgetting about all of the boats the lighthouse touches with its light every day! focus on your boats... the ones that need and love and support what you do.)

you are here to connect with others, to communicate, to share yourself and your stories and the light that lives inside.

being a beacon is about being visible. it's about raising your voice. being seen & being heard and saying: hey world, this is me.

ways to be a beacon include: sharing your stories, getting on your soapbox, having a signature thing that you are known for, helping others, listening to others, being vulnerable and making genuine connections with others.

the beacon is all about authenticity, communication, connection, and owning your voice.

it's about sharing you.

share you.

your light is not meant to be hidden inside, you are meant to share YOU with others... this is about standing tall and saying 'hey world, this is me!' and remember, when you do the authentic, vulnerable thing, that is where amazing things happen!

what is one area in life that you have been hiding you... some way you have been dimming your light or keeping a part of you quiet or unseen?	**who** could you share this with? consider: friends, spouse, children, family members, groups, networks, forums, mastermind (create your own?)	**how** can you share more of you? ideas: write, art, sing, dance, photos, events, speak, teach, present, blog, social media, youtube, podcast

your comfort zone.

our ability to speak up and be seen is related to our comfort zone... just imagine a target with expanding circles of visibility and comfort, related to WHAT we share, HOW we share, and WHO we share it with. when we leap far out of our comfort zone we trigger our fear! try starting with what feels safe and comfy... start at the centre and work outwards from there. remember to keep pushing outwards to new levels... what was once scary soon becomes comfy!

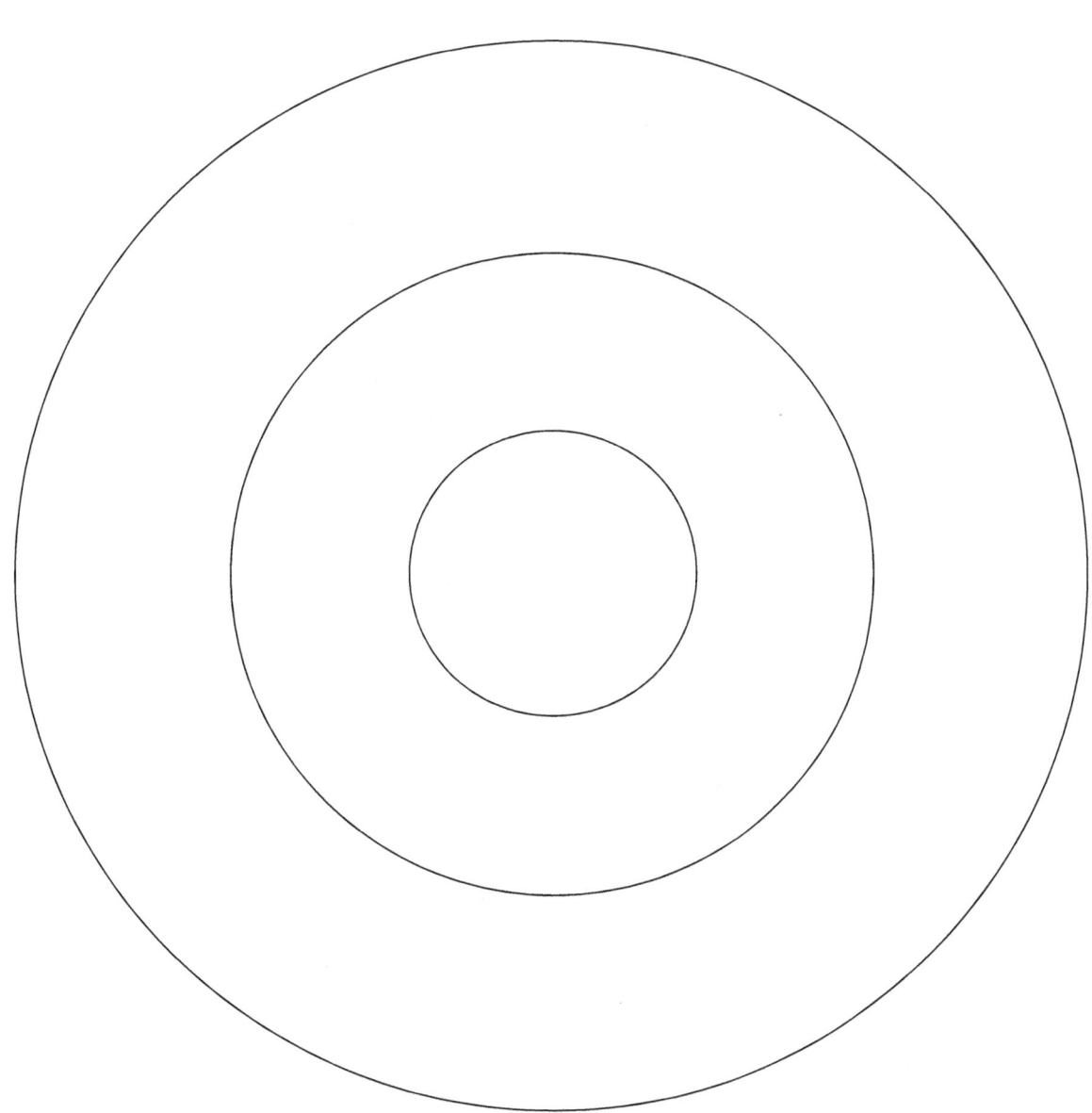

your story.

sharing your story is a powerful way to speak your truth, to own who you are. your story heals you. it allows you to connect with others... giving them permission to share their story, to shine their light.

what **stories** have shaped you? AHA moments, sliding doors moments, turning points, failures, successes, challenges, encounters

what is the one thing you care about deeply & passionately? (maybe there are a few things that fit under one umbrella!) your fight song, your soap box, your **mission**, what you stand for...

what are you learning yourself that you wish to share with others? something you can't help but **teach** to others? what is resonating with you right now in a big way that you might share?

when you share your stories, your fight song, your lessons... what always seems to **resonate** with others? when do people tell you: wow, me too! or: thank you for sharing that!

your signature thing.

*your signature thing is about knowing you & being you, being fully seen & heard in a bold way... and owning it! it's about being known for something. what do you want to be known for? what is your own personal *tattoo* that you display to the world?*

describe **you**:
loves/obsessions
favourite things
colours, shapes,
patterns, symbols,
words, phrases,
inspired by...
drawn towards...
value deeply...

describe **your vibe**:
quirky, funny, playful
sweet, sensitive, kind,
strong, passionate,
calm, organized,
active, motivating,
energetic, wild
knowing, observant,
thoughtful, simple

you do you **express** it?
fashion, accessories,
hair, nails, makeup,
décor, objects,
collections,
words, phrases,
interests, hobbies,
music, art,
activities

how can you **amplify** it?
own it in a bigger way
be known as the _____ lady
make it your signature thing

navigate | 53

your manifesto.

a manifesto can be an awesome way to get clear on what matters to you, to own it by sharing it with the world, and to connect with others who care about the same things you do. it can also become a filter for you going forward, helping you make decisions, grow, & evolve. write your personal manifesto, a biz or career manifesto, a manifesto for your home or community, anything at all! try these prompts:

i **believe** in

my **wish** for the world is

above all else i **stand** for

my ultimate **goal** is

i have a **dream**

if i could **share** just one thing, it is

if there is one thing i could **change** it would be

i am on a **mission**/quest/adventure to

you are not **alone**

you are doing a **good job**

it's going to be **ok**

this is my **promise**

once you have some ideas, you can put them together in a fun way that feels like you. try: a poster, a shareable image, a video, slideshow, doodle, poem, mantra, collage, cartoon, booklet, or ebook.

your connections.

you can't be all things to all people... you can't please everyone. focus on your boats... those people who see your light. who are your boats? who will you focus on creating connections with?

who are your **supporters**, cheerleaders, champions, and fans?	who do you **long to help**? who would feel better/less along just by knowing you?
challenge: say thank you. let them know about your plans and ideas for the year.	**challenge**: connect with them. ask how they are doing. listen.
who **"gets" you**? has similar interests, values, passions, spark, outlook, etc.	who do you have a **girl crush** on? who inspires, teaches, motivates you?
challenge: make time to meet up and connect, perhaps a coffee date, fb group, skype chat, etc.	**challenge**: follow them. thank them for influencing and inspiring you.

Make like a Lighthouse and Shine

have only one rule.
be your wild,
courageous,
brilliant self.
every single day.
no matter what.

leigh stanley

build your tower

the tower of the lighthouse represents the life that you are actually building for yourself... it's the structure or the vehicle that allows you to be you and to shine your light in the world.

and the fact is that we all have a structure that we have built for ourselves already, without even realizing it.

our lives are full of all sorts of *stuff* - work and relationships and activities and strategies and belongings and obligations and hobbies and interests and people and jobs and physical spaces and and and....

some of it wonderful, some of it perhaps not quite so.

the lighthouse reminds us to build a tower.

something which is in alignment with who you are – with your purpose and your BIG vision, something that will leverage your strengths and your passions, something with strength and integrity where every component belongs.

for everything in our lives we must ask: how's this working out for me? does this serve me? does this feel like me? does this light me up? if not... can you change it, change the way you think about it, definite it differently, declutter it, make space for something new?

what you are building has to match who you are. it needs to serve you well.

the tower is all about alignment, integrity, simplicity, priority, and leverage.

it's about serving you.

serve you.

check your tower right now: surroundings, to do lists, tasks, jobs, obligations, activities, strategies, plans, people, belongings, stuff... ask: is this working for me? check for alignment, integrity, simplicity...

list what's in your tower	how well is that **serving** you?	what do you need to **do now**?

your tower

what do you want in your tower? you are the architect of your ideal lighthouse... choose wisely!

rules. what rules have you been telling yourself? ask: who says? write your own rules!	**boundaries.** decide: what is ok for you... what is a yes, what is a no...
rooms. what have you been locking away in a room? make time for the stuff that calls to you.	**doors.** open your doors to abundance... to giving and receiving in return! "i serve, i deserve."
currency. where do you want to spend your time, energy, focus, thoughts, money?	**space.** what would you like to allow into your tower (people, learning, opportunities)?

navigate | 67

your permission.

permission is one of the most important tools to build a tower... to build a life... that feels aligned and serves us well. give yourself permission to make a change, to say yes/no, to declutter, to prioritize... to build what YOU love... and to build it YOUR way.

i give myself **permission** to...

your definitions.

you know what you want for yourself... now is the time to define it clearly... to write new definitions that are the perfect fit. define your goals, desires, roles, titles, etc. pick a few words that are important to you... use the ideas below or choose your own words to define... open up the thesaurus to find better words, or invent your own!

success
rich
healthy
impact
fun
joy
play
creativity
adventure
peace
growth
independent
fulfilled
freedom
generous
curious
simplicity
alignment
integrity
vulnerable
strong
brave
worthy
confident
intuitive
ignited
leader
friend
partner
family
boss
entrepreneur
team
colleague
volunteer
coach
teacher

your focus.

our tower can be filled up with so many things... part of our job as the architect of our life is to choose our priorities, to decide where our focus goes, to decide what strategies/plans/steps will actually best serve the intentions we hold for ourselves. consider what you most want for you... what 3 things will you focus on? choose 3 most important actions (MIA's) or 3 areas in your life/work as your priorities.

#1

#2

#3

your sacred space.

treat your physical world as a sacred space that represents the tower of your lighthouse. what are you surrounded by? what is the energy like in your space? how does it make you feel? how do you WANT it to make you feel? are you surrounding yourself with light igniters or light extinguishers? who are your fellow lighthouse keepers? can you create a physical sacred space to helps you feel ignited and stay focused? this could be a space in your home that you make yours... a room, a corner, even a wall!

what would your **dream sacred space** look like? can you **start creating it**, even in small steps, now?

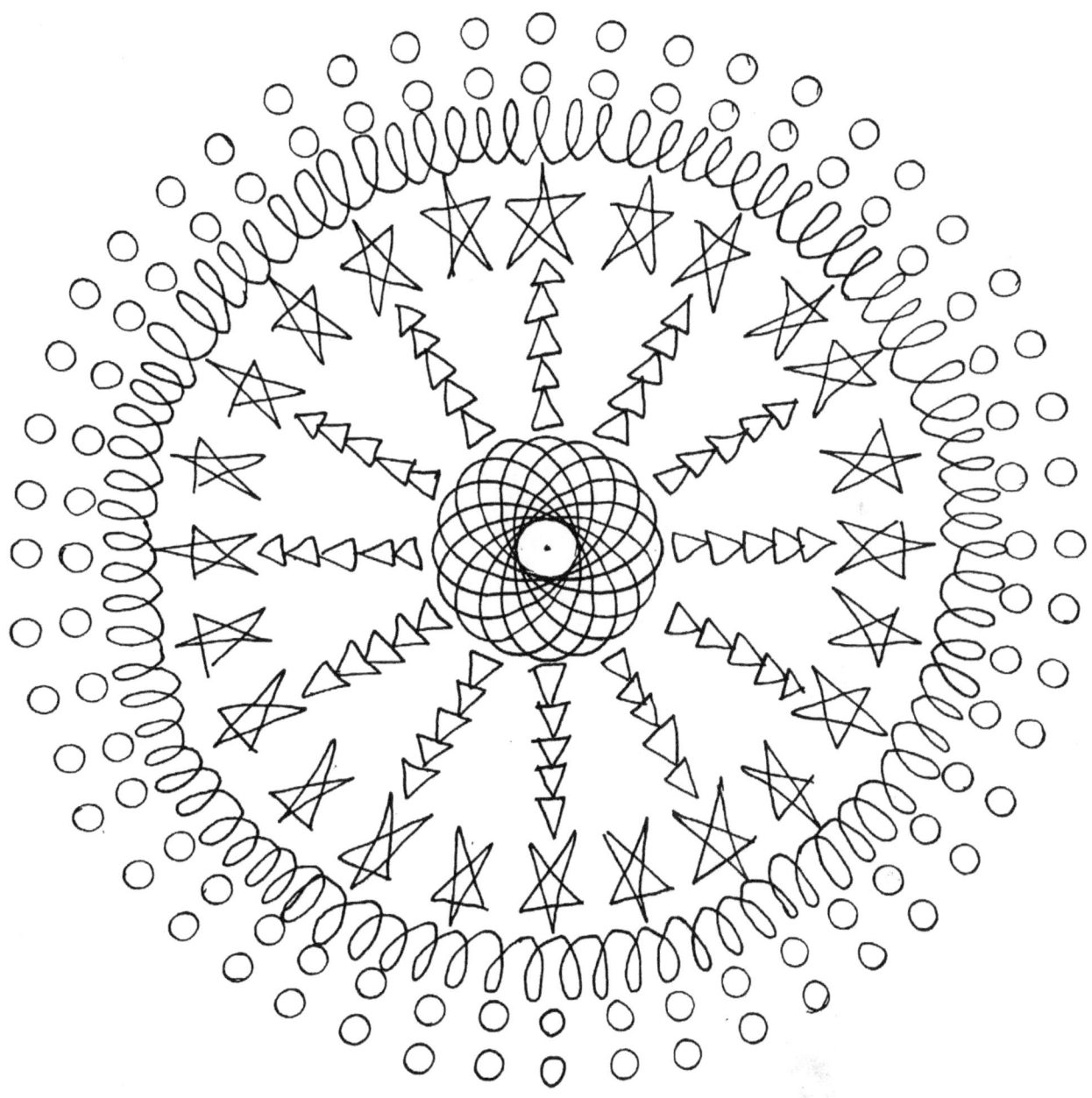

believe in yourself
and all that you are.
know that there is
something inside you
that is greater than
any obstacle.

christian d. larson

strengthen your foundation

another component of the lighthouse that we must remember to build is the foundation.

the foundation of the lighthouse is there to strengthen and support the entire structure above... the tower, the beacon, the beautiful light.

the foundation is the ground you build on... the rock... it needs to be solid, stable, and strong, in order to support you as do the work you are here to do, as you build the life you want to build, and shine the light you are here to shine.

building your foundation means building yourself up.

each building block of the foundation is a part of your *mindset*: confidence, worthiness, self-belief, commitment, courage, resilience, tenacity, self-love, positive attitude, positive self-talk, action taking, risk taking, decision making, instincts, certainty, consistency...

... all of the inner stuff we need in order to stand tall and stand out and shine our light.

some foundation building blocks come naturally to us, we can cement them in and make quick use of the them. others we need to build on purpose

just as we build any other aspect of our lives, our plans, our dreams... we need to build up ourselves too. a strong foundation doesn't just magically appear when we start to shine our light, we must build this too.

the foundation is all about support, strength, taking action, and standing tall.

it's about building you.

your foundation.

take a look at that list of the parts of mindset that make up our foundation (on the previous page)...

i naturally have these as part of my mindset (and now i can **strengthen** them)

i know that i need to **build** these parts of my mindset (and i can look for strategies to help me!)

i am removing these old, wobbly bits (stories, experiences, evidence) that make my foundation weak...

your responsibility.

so many of us allow our mindset... our confidence, our worthiness, our belief, our ability to take action, our resilience, even our happiness... to depend on other people or other things. we come up with excuses and conditions and reasons and blame as to why we aren't, or why we can't. "i will take action when..." "i will feel confident when..." "i'm not enough because..." we are still looking for a boss or a report card to or a university to tell us we are ready. it's time to take responsibility... to say enough is enough... i AM enough... **my ability to stand tall depends on me, you are off the hook.**

what is the old excuse you have been telling yourself?

my _____ depends on me. _____ you are off the hook.
           (mindset)   (excuse)

my _____ depends on me. _____ you are off the hook.
           (mindset)   (excuse)

my _____ depends on me. _____ you are off the hook.
           (mindset)   (excuse)

your certainty.

one of the biggest indicators of success is belief in yourself, confidence in your abilities, certainty that it WILL happen... but it is hard to believe in something that feels like it is just a dream. the certainty game will help you build belief in yourself by little increments (instead of big leaps!) here's how you play:

use the grid and start in the first box with **"what i know for sure!"** keep that certainty in mind then jump ahead one spot: if *that* is true, what happens next? and then what happens? and then what would be the result of that? keep asking yourself **"and then what?"** until you get closer to the **BIG vision** you hold for yourself. try to keep that feeling (that certainty) of what you know for sure in mind as you go.

your action taking.

we all feel stuck sometimes... procrastinating, waiting, making excuses, not really trying very hard to do the thing we say we want to do. but we can actually learn to be better action takers...

it's not a tattoo. it's ok if you get it wrong, if you change your mind, if you are unsure. just start now and change it when you need to. what could you just try? (knowing you can change it?)

take imperfect action on purpose... so that you can learn as you go, can figure out the next steps, ca test or try or explore. what are you hoping to learn as you go?

done is better than perfect. no one else knows the picture of perfection you hold for yourself, it only exists in your head. where could you stop judging yourself against a picture no one else can see?

JFDI (just fucking do it.) don't wait another moment. the time will never be right, you will never be ready/good enough. one year from now what will you be so glad you started today?

back yourself. fight for what you say you want for yourself. if your best friend was procrastinating what would you say to them? fight just as hard for you as you would for your best friend.

your mindset.

let's practice building some other aspects of our mindset...

belief. when someone tells you they love you believe them! what has someone told you recently?

worthiness. claim your worth. celebrate your successes, achievements, strengths, and gifts!

focus. what you focus on expands. what thoughts, beliefs, evidence do you choose to focus on now?

resilience. if you fall/fail it's not the end of the world. what might be the silver lining?

abundance. when was the last time you felt lucky? blessed? abundant? remember that feeling!

courage. what was the last brave thing you did? why did you feel brave? what was the result?

another one? what mindset do you need to build? how do you think you could start today?

your rituals.

a ritual is simply something that reminds us to be present in the moment. you likely have many rituals already - they just might not be serving you well, they might be keeping you in a stuck place. create your own rituals, daily practice, weekly/monthly routines... anything that will help you to take care of you, connect to your light, strengthen your foundation. here are some places you might already have rituals... can you tweak them to better serve you, replace old rituals with new ones, make your rituals more fun?

- start day
- end day
- start work
- end work
- start week
- end week
- weekend
- start month
- end month
- start year
- end year
- holidays
- meal times
- break times
- other?

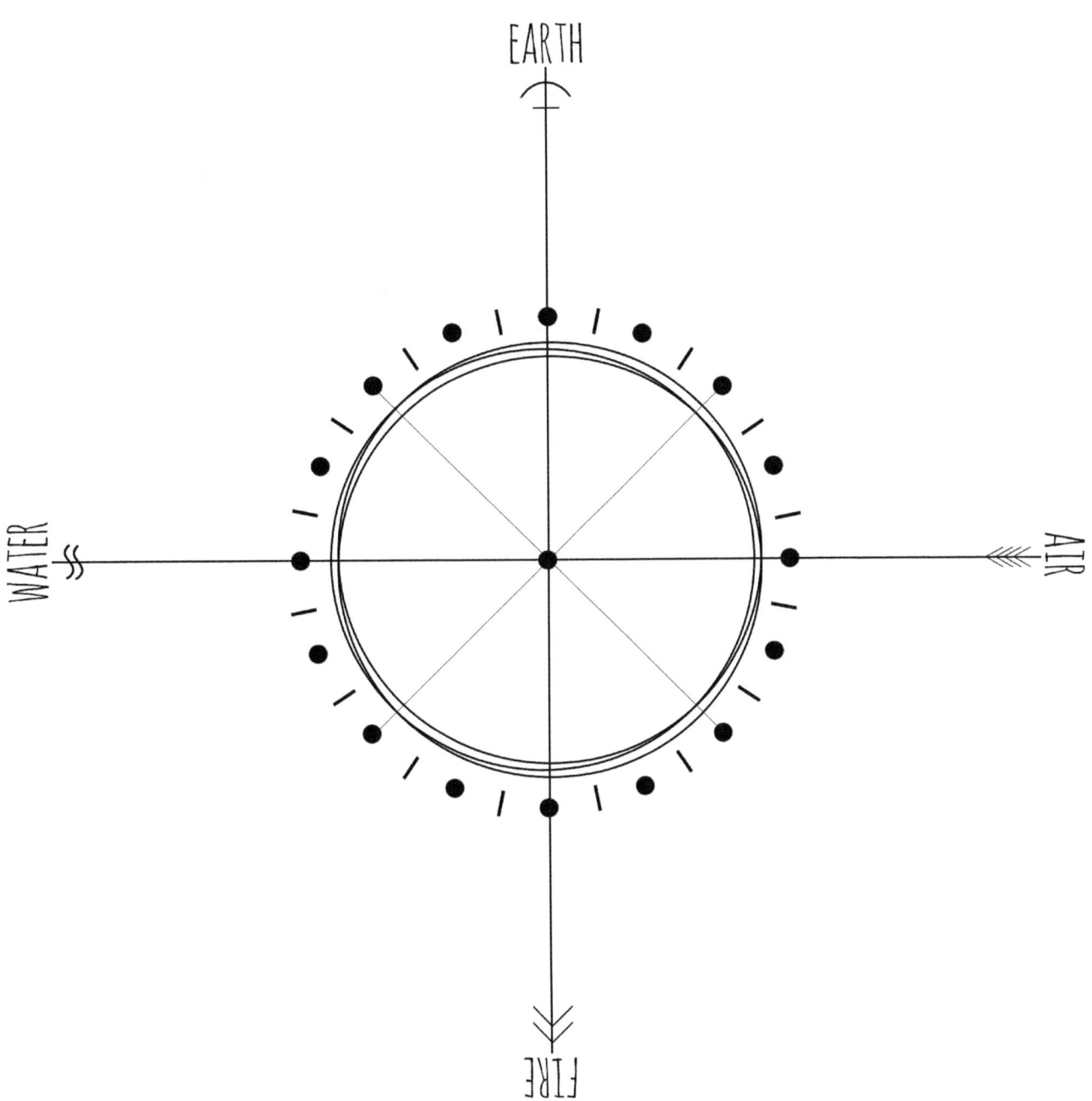

the jump is so frightening
between where i am
and where i want to be...
because of all i may become,
i will close my eyes and leap.

mary ann hershey

use the spiral staircase

the spiral staircase of the lighthouse is a beautiful reminder that you are simply on a journey.

every step you take, takes you closer to the top of the lighthouse – to your goal, your dream, your BIG vision, your purpose. and even though, as you are climbing those steps, it may seem like you are going round and round and not getting anywhere...

but if you picture that staircase from above, it is a beautiful spiral. when you look at it that way, each step is taking you closer to the centre as well. to your core. to who you are in this world and the work you are meant to be doing... your light that you are meant to shine.

with each step you take the next steps appear. every little step takes you closer to the top AND to your centre. you aren't going around in circles. it's a spiral. made of tiny little steps... which are easy to climb.

so just keep marching on. keep climbing.

deal with any stuff that comes up, don't let it get you stuck. stuck stuff can include: frustration, criticism, shame, guilt, worry, doubt, fear, overwhelm, jealousy, comparison, dejection, inner critic, bad attitude, failure, anger, etc.

this stuff is simply part of the journey... it comes up for a reason, for you to grow and explore and evolve, and part of your job is to face it, to get unstuck, and to keep going!

the spiral staircase is about feeling empowered, rising above, getting unstuck, and taking the journey. it's about honouring the journey.... because you are exactly where you are meant to be.

it's about honouring you.

awareness.

shine a light of awareness on the stuff that holds you back, keeps you small, or makes you question this path... that's how it begins to lose its power!

fear. what is your biggest fear? let it play out. if that happens, then what? and then what?

inner critic. what does that voice tell you? in what way is it trying to keep you safe & small?

fog. what thoughts, beliefs, doubts, cloud up your windows, stop you from seeing yourself clearly?

stuckness. what else has you feeling stuck? (jealousy, comparison, frustration, worry, overwhelm?.)

responses. what are your 'go to ' excuses, defences, judgements, responses to this stuck stuff?

secrets. what is the secret, unseen stuff you keep locked inside, hidden away from the world?

understanding.

spiral with your stuff... look at your "stuckness" with a sense of curiosity and wonder... ask "hmmmm... i wonder what's really going on here?"

often, when something has us feeling stuck or triggered (or angry, or frustrated, or annoyed), it is coming up because there is something we are meant to learn about and work on within ourselves. think about your stuck situation and then "hold up a mirror" and consider: what is being reflected back on you.

for example if you are not feeling supported by someone else, where do you need to support yourself? how can you do that? if someone is criticising you, where are you being critical of yourself? and how can you change that?

what has you feeling **stuck**?	what is that **reflecting back to you**?

navigate

clearing.

one powerful way to clear and to heal the stuck stuff that blocks your path on this journey is forgiveness.

---

choose one of the "stuck" things that has come up for you in this guidebook.
list all of your memories, feelings, thoughts, patterns, stories, beliefs, etc. about it this situation...

ho'opnopono:
i love you. i am sorry. please forgive me. thank you.

---

visualize each one of those things you noted, or picture the whole situation in your mind's eye. shower yourself with love, compassion, and forgiveness... and say this mantra until you feel the energy clear. (feel free to adapt this mantra – but the thing to remember is this: this is about clearing your stuff. you cannot change anyone else! forgiveness is about healing you, so that you can move on.)

reframing.

another way of shifting the energy of the "stuck stuff" is to reframe it. flip your thinking and turn the negative stuff (fears, doubts, beliefs, thoughts, etc.) into something positive. when you catch yourself in the negative "switch the station" and play something positive in your head instead! instead of letting something stop you or hold you back... let it show you the way forward! give your 'stuff' a new job.

who am i to....	who am i NOT to....
i am so jealous of...	it's a sign! it's my turn next!
i have no time...	it matters to me, i'm going to make time.

fun.

spiralling with your stuff doesn't have to be tough, hard, horrible work. it's simply part of the journey... so change your attitude towards it! have some FUN with your stuck stuff with one of these strategies...

curiosity hmmmmmm.... i wonder about...	**question** what am i here to learn from...
explore let's see... what could be going on here...	**predict** i predict what will happen next...
joy oh wow! this is coming up for a reason...	**play** make it a game... shout bingo when...

your tools.

even with great mindset strategies, it can still feel like there is a big wall in front of us that we just can't move past. how else could you clear or heal or shift the energy of the stuckness... the resistance, blocks, obstacles... you are experiencing?

for instance: EFT, kinesiology, reiki, art therapy, journaling, talking (therapist, coach, mentor, spiritual advisor), meditation/prayer, intuitive help, essential oils, feng shui, physical movement/exercise, etc.

whatever you choose to try: have a genuine willingness and clear intention to shift the blocks in your way, try combining tools to create your own clearing techniques, and be sure to follow up by taking inspired, courageous action.

my tool belt of strategies to clear stuff energetically, emotionally, physically, and mentally.

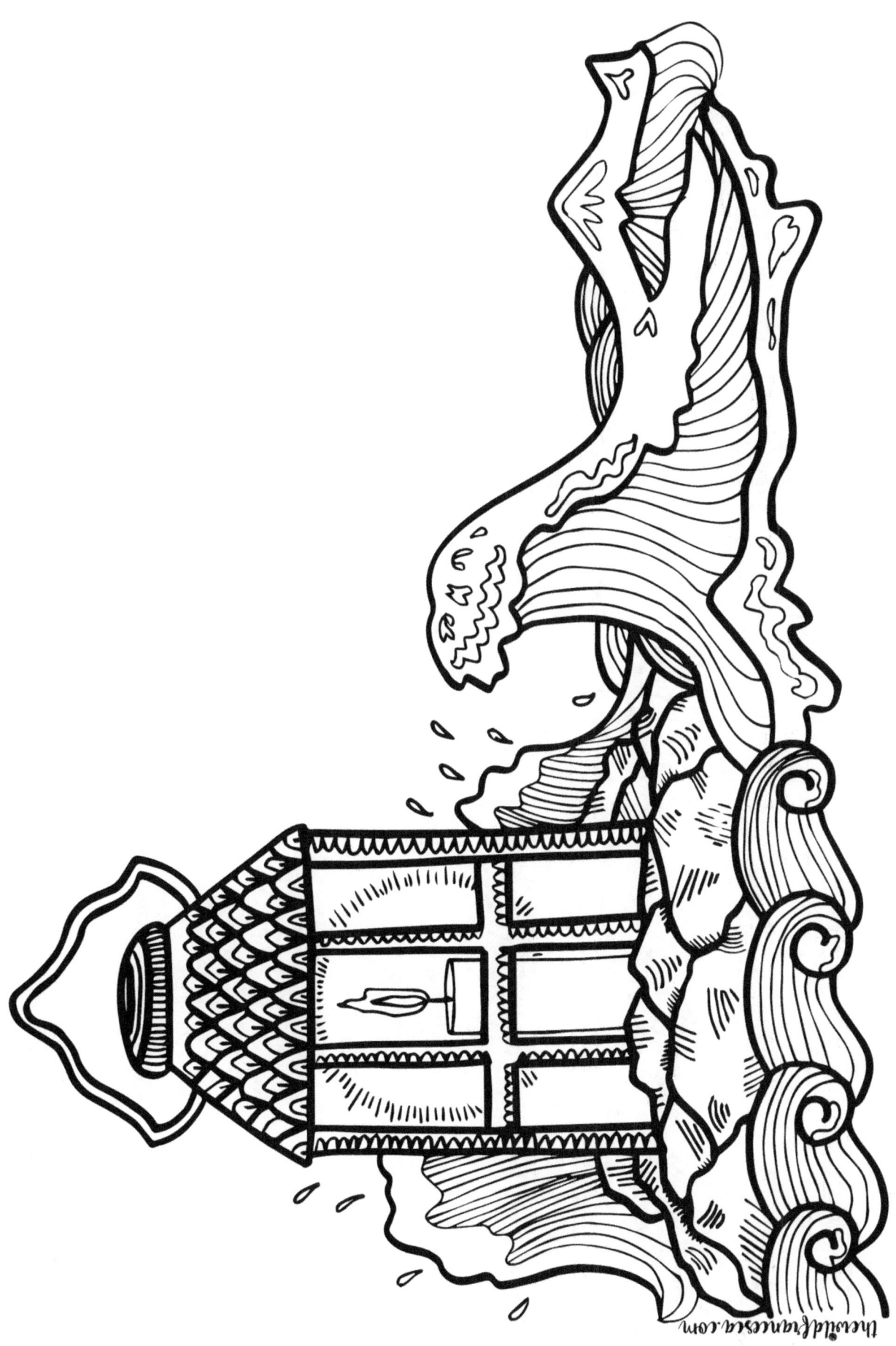

only when we are
brave enough
to explore the
darkness
will we discover
the infinite power
of our light.

brene brown

find your harbour

building a lighthouse isn't a do once thing. you will always be working at shining your light, and sometimes things won't feel so shiny an bright.

we all experience some darkness... stormy weather... massive tides. we need to honour this, if this is where we are at. and we can learn from it, grow from the place we are at... for our biggest challenges, our deepest wounds... these are our greatest gifts. this is the place our light can enter.

the harbour reminds us that we can come back to the lighthouse any time... we can come back inside and do a bit more work... we can come back home.

the harbour is a safe haven, when it feels like the waves are crashing in, when we feel lost at sea, or perhaps like we are sinking.

our own lighthouse will be a beacon to us, a guiding light reminding us that everything will be alright, and pointing the way back home. it helps us to remember we are surrounded by an ocean of love.

the harbour is all about safety, security, belonging, grounding, and space.

it's about coming back to you.

your darkness.

the reality is that we are not going to live in the light all of the time... we will also experience times of darkness. remember, the darkness is the gateway to your light... you need to feel your way through to the other side. so honour where you are at... it is exactly where you are meant to be.

what is the biggest **challenge** for you right now, the deepest wound or darkest depths?	where does it feel like you are merely watching from the sidelines or standing in the **shadows**?
in what way do you feel like you've been tossed around by crazy **highs and lows**?	where do you feel like you are always **efforting** and never getting anywhere?

your come back rate.

how do we find our way through the darkness, the shadows, the storms, and the tides? we come back home... to our harbour, to our light. here are some strategies that can help with that...

grounding. be where your feet are... bring your mind and your focus to the here and now.

gratitude. look around you... think about your journey so far. what are you grateful for?

a new day. tomorrow is a new invitation to shine. what can you do to accept that invitation?

surrender. sometimes we need to let go of all that stuff we are hanging onto. what could you do physically or symbolically to surrender today... to set yourself free.

space. space creates flow. what feels like space to you? what could you do to create a little space?

belonging.

a sense of belonging & support is a powerful tool to come back to your harbour. remember: you are surrounded by an ocean of love!

what **community** (online or off) feels like home to you?	who are your **lighthouse keepers**, the ones who see your light clearly & help you keep shining?
are you seeking any other support to **weather the storms**?	how can you regularly connect with your **supporters**?

safety.

it's incredibly difficult to do ANY of the things in any part of your lighthouse if you don't feel safe. have a think about some of the things you have worked on here... seeing yourself clearly, sharing yourself authentically, giving yourself permission, building your mindset, spiralling with your stuckness... and think about where you need to feel safe. try writing a series of statements to remind you that it's safe.

it is safe to...

your anchor.

what do you want for yourself? what is your intention? an anchor helps you to come back to your light, to the high vibe feeling of being ignited. tweak this practice however it suits you, eg: start each day or week or month or project with an intention & choose an anchor for it! have specific anchors for the different areas of your life/home/work etc.

a word.

who you are, what you want, your big dreams... what do they all add up to? think of one word that summarizes your intention. choose a word that feels powerful, inspiring! post it somewhere visible so you can be reminded of it every day. use your word as a guiding light... to make decisions, to keep focused, to stay inspired.

a talisman.

choose a talisman or a symbol that physically represents your intention. you could choose an animal totem, a crystal stone or other object, a signature scent or essential oil, a colour, a number, a piece of jewellery... anything really! something you could hold, wear, or display... like a touchstone that reminds you of your light.

a theme song.

have a written or visual representation of your intention. choose a song... or if you'd rather, choose a mantra, a quote, a book, a movie, a person or character, a photograph etc. that embodies your intention. something you can say or sing or picture to remind you of your light, and get you pumped up and ready to shine when you need it.

your walls.

you've been exploring a lot of stuff in this guidebook... and it's so important to NOT let the negative stuff become permanent graffiti on our walls... instead, please write on your walls with love. use this space to include positive statements, affirmations, celebrations, reminders of your purpose, your why, your gifts... and more! find a physical space in your home or office to display these reminders. add to them often!

write on your walls with love.

you are the servant
of something
much bigger than you,
something
fucking unstoppable.

gabrielle bernstein

look up at the sky

when you look up at the sky above be reminded that you are a part of something much bigger than any one person... something that is the source of all light.

you decide what that means to you: call it your soul or intuition or higher self; angels or guides; god or spirit or divine or the universe... or simply just *source*.

the key is to have faith. create a belief in a connection to something bigger than you, a belief that you are guided on this journey. trust that the universe has your back. trust that you are exactly where you are meant to be, trust that you can take a leap, and the road will rise up to meet you.

you get to connect to source in whatever way that makes sense to you... you get to do spirituality your way... when you do, it does make a difference to your journey. a spiritual practice takes a weight off your shoulders, it injects a feeling of hope and belief, it allows you to connect to whatever lights you up.

you connect to your light by being the light... tapping into the high vibration energy of love, joy, peace, inspiration, growth, and authenticity. you get to do that in any way you choose... what feels like *light* to you?

your light doesn't come *from* you, it comes *through* you. you are simply a channel, a vehicle, for light. your job is to show up, rise up, light up, and shine.

the sky is about spirituality, guidance, faith, and trust.

it's about connecting to you.

your intuition.

intuition is the way you connect to your inner light... to your inner wisdom or higher self. we all have it, some of us just don't know it well or don't connect to it as much as we like. you can build up your intuition, become more aware of how your particular intuition works, and practice using it in your life.

when was a time you **listened** to your intuition? didn't listen to your intuition? what happened?	how does your intuition **work**? (a feeling, a body sensation, words/messages, signs/images, etc.)
what would you like some intuitive **guidance** on right now? (in your life, self, work, home, wherever!)	now **notice** what happens. play. have fun! make a game of it, like a treasure hunt searching for clues!

try starting a notebook to keep track of your intuitive 'hits' - what you notice and how it works. it's like strengthening a muscle! try saying out loud: thank you, that was awesome! please, more like that!

your spirituality.

spirituality is simply how you connect to the source of your light – and you get to do you, you get to think about it any way you like. if walking on the beach feels like connection to you, that is awesome. if you aren't sure... try to be open to exploring and playing with what would feel like connection to you!

do you have any **past experience** with spirituality (memories, rules you were told, beliefs that were pressed on you) that you would like to embrace, heal, or clear?

what is **your version** of spirituality? in what way do you feel connected or guided? how can you tap into that connection? what helps you to have faith, belief, trust?

what would an ideal **spiritual practice** look like to you? how can you fit more of that into your daily & weekly practice? what would you like to explore or play with?

your universe.

it can help you feel connected to your light to remember that you are a part of something much bigger than you... something that is unstoppable. it's not actually all about you... sometimes you have to 'get over yourself' and just show up and shine your light, because it is what you are here to do. you are here to be one star in a sky full of light... you are here to add your 'book' to the universe's 'library'.

in what way are you a part of something that is **bigger than you**...
what might happen if you just **show up and shine** and stop worrying, stop waiting...
what does **you shining your light** add something to the universe...

your vibes.

it's really hard to feel connected to your light when you are in a low vibe place... we need to be the energy we wish to receive. meditation is one way that people choose to let go of all of the low vibe stuff and get to a more connected, high vibe place... but it is not the only way! you can raise your vibes and connect to your light even in the simplest of moments... and you can choose to add more of these moments to your day. have a think about the moments that you feel most in the high vibe energy of light: peace, love, joy, inspiration, space, mindfulness, flow, authenticity... connection.

- walking
- creating
- helping
- laughter
- moving
- playing
- dancing
- serving
- listening
- looking
- driving
- music
- shower
- yoga
- running
- colouring
- drawing
- touching
- journaling
- breathing

navigate | 143

lighthouses don't go
running all over an island
looking for boats to save;
they just stand there
shining.

anne lamott

make like a lighthouse and shine.

use the lighthouse image, on the previous page, to jot down any things you want to remember or keep fresh in your mind about building your lighthouse and navigating back to your light.

use the quotes in this guidebook to inspire you on your journey... and add your own quotes/mantras/lyrics to these pages to remind you of the light that you are here to shine.

use the colouring in pages for more inspiration, brainstorming, organizing your ideas, even for tracking your progress with your intentions!

and come back to these exercises whenever you are feeling like you need to work on building your lighthouse... truthfully, the work is never done!

as you build your lighthouse – as you rise up and stand tall, light up and shine bright, we would love to have you join the lighthouse revolution.

visit karengunton.com to join and receive access a variety of free ideas & inspiration to help you navigate your journey and shine your light.

be sure to join the free #lighthouserevolution community group on facebook: ask questions, share what you are working on, share your ideas, and meet like-minded lighthouse keepers... we are here to be part of your ocean of support.

facebook.com/groups/lighthouserevolution

see you there...

and keep shining!

it's what you were born to do.

thank you to the following contributors
for the inspiring art work included in this guidebook:

"the light points to my true north"~ barbara laskey ~ instagram.com/barbartist2000

"navigate" ~ vanisha lalchandani

"star mandala" ~ taylor gunton ~ age 9

"the lantern & the sea" ~ nicole tripp ~ thewildfrancesca.com

karen gunton is a teacher, author, and speaker on self-leadership strategies for being your highest, brightest self and living a life that lights you up.

she is also a badass rule-breaker who never uses capitals... she believes in giving yourself permission to be you, to own your light, and shine your way.

karen started the lighthouse revolution as part of her mission to inspire women to rise up, stand tall, get ignited, clear the fog, and start shining... just like a lighthouse.

she lives in adelaide, australia with her husband and three children... though, every australian winter she chases the sun back to canada for more summer fun. you can find her in her happy place: on the beach with a book in one hand, a cold beer in the other, and her bare toes in the sand.

find karen on facebook, instagram, and twitter @karengunton or at her website karengunton.com where you will find free resources and a free community for the lighthouse revolution.

karen also offers a variety of online workshops, group programs, and personal sessions to help women learn tools for self-leadership and building a lighthouse in their business or their life. karen is available as a keynote speaker, and/or workshop presenter for live events.